RENGETSU

Life and Poetry of Lotus Moon

Rengetsu

Life and Poetry of Lotus Moon

Translation and Biography by
JOHN STEVENS

ECHO POINT BOOKS & MEDIA, LLC

Some of the translations herein first appeared in
Lotus Moon: The Poetry of Rengetsu published by White Pine Press.
These translations are used with permission.
White Pine Press also publishes two other translations by John Stevens:
Wild Ways: Zen Poems of Ikkyu and *Mountain Tasting: Haiku & Journals of Santoka Taneda.*
www.WhitePinePress.org

Cover art: *Plum Tree with Calligraphy* by Otagaki Rengetsu
Courtesy of
The Private Collection of Dr. John Fong and Dr. Colin Johnstone
www.RengetsuZenCollections.com

Published by Echo Point Books & Media
www.EchoPointBooks.com

ISBN: 978-1-62654-931-9

Book design by Adrienne Nunez,
Echo Point Books & Media

Editorial and proofreading assistance by Christine Schultz,
Echo Point Books & Media

Printed in the U.S.A.

Otagaki Rengetsu in her hut in Nishigamo

CONTENTS

FEATURED ARTWORK

The Life of OTAGAKI RENGETSU

EARLY YEARS

Otagaki Rengetsu was born on the eighth day of the first month of Keisei III (1791) in the Sanbogi pleasure district of Kyoto. She was the love child of an unnamed courtesan and Todo Kinshichiro Yoshikiyo (1767–1798), a high ranking retainer of Iga Ueno Castle. Within a few days of her birth, she was adopted by Otagaki Teruhisa[1] and his wife Nawa. They named her Nobu. In August of the same year, Teruhisa was appointed sacristan of Chion-in, the

---

[1] In her two-page autobiography, Rengetsu reads the characters of his name 光古 as "Mitsuhisa." However, those characters can also be read "Teruhisa." Other references call him Teruhisa but give the characters 輝古. Japanese names can be read in many different ways depending on the circumstances. It is a very confusing practice. As in almost all sources, Teruhisa is the name used in this account.

huge headquarter temple of the Jodo Sect. Both the adoption and Teruhisa's appointment were likely arranged by Nobu's natural father Yoshikiyo.

Nobu had an older stepbrother named Katahisa. The four other children of Teruhisa and Nawa, all male, had died previously at early ages. When Nobu reached six years of age,[2] her parents started schooling her in literature and poetry, and her father gave her basic instruction in swordplay. Since Teruhisa was well known as a *go* player, he introduced Nobu to the challenging game at a young age. She eventually became a very skillful *go* player.

Nobu was raised in the religious atmosphere of Chion-in. The primary practice of the Jodo Sect is *nembutsu*, which is the constant repetition of the name of Amida Butsu. This deity is the Buddha of the Pure Land who vows to save everyone who sincerely calls upon his name. In her childhood from morning to night, Nobu was surrounded by the chant, *Namu Amida Butsu.*

In 1798 at age eight, Nobu was called to serve as a lady-in-waiting at Kameoka Castle. This summons

---

[2] All ages are reckoned Japanese-style that considers a person one year old at birth. Since there are discrepancies in the various accounts of Rengetsu's life, the dates given here (with the exception of her death) are approximate.

may have been at the request of her natural father Yoshikiyo. Since there was a close connection between Iga Ueno Castle and Kameoka Castle, Yoshikiyo may have wanted Nobu to go there for a samurai education. Another theory is that Nobu's birth mother was living at Kameoka Castle, and she wanted to be with her daughter. Whatever the case may have been, during her nine-year stay at the castle, Nobu learned proper deportment, was drilled in the martial arts, and she was also educated in the arts of calligraphy, literature, poetry, tea ceremony, flower arranging, and dancing. Nobu became exceptionally adept in the use of *jujutsu* and handling the halberd, the sword, and the *kusarigama* (sickle and chain). She may have also practiced *ninjutsu*. The Iga Clan of Yoshikiyo was famous for the many *ninja* in its ranks and *ninjutsu* may well have been part of the martial art curriculum of Kameoka Castle. By the age of 17, Nobu was held to be at the level of *menkyo-kaiden* (teaching license) in the martial arts.

During her stay at the castle, Nobu was hit by the first of many tragedies—in 1803, when she was 13 years old, both her stepbrother (age 21) and her stepmother (age 44) passed away.

MARRIAGE AND
THE PAIN OF CHILDBIRTH

In 1807, Nobu completed her service at Kameoka
Castle and returned home to Chion-in. It had been
arranged for her to marry. A few years before, Oka
(Tayuinosho) Tenzo had been adopted into the
Otagaki family assuming the name Mochihisa. Since
Nobu had met Mochihisa a few times when she was
serving in the castle, her betrothal to him was not
unexpected.

In 1808, her first son, Tetsutaro, was born in
October. He died less than a month later. In Sep-
tember 1810, her first daughter Tanshin was born.
Tanshin died in December of 1812. In June of 1815,
Nobu's second daughter Chie was born. Chie died
within a few days after birth.

Mochihisa was evidently not much of a husband, spending most of his time in dissipation, gambling, drinking, and chasing women. Nobu separated from him soon after the birth (and death) of their second daughter Chie in 1815. The ailing Mochihisa returned to his hometown and died in August of the same year.

In 1819, at the age of 29, Nobu married Ishikawa Jujiro, who was adopted into the Otagaki family as Hisatoshi, and he was given a post at Chion-in. Nobu's third daughter Chigyoku was born at the end of the same year. The union between Nobu and Hisatoshi was happy. However, tragedy struck again. Hisatoshi died of illness on June 19th, 1823. The night before, 33-year-old old Nobu shaved her head, vowing to renounce the world. A few days later, Nobu formally took vows as a Pure Land Buddhist nun, assuming the name Rengetsu, "Lotus Moon." At the same time, her father Teruhisa became a priest under the name of Saishin, "Pure Land Heart." Soon after his ordination, Saishin (Teruhisa) turned over his position at Chion-in to yet another adopted son, Hisaatsu, and retired.

Saishin, Rengetsu, and her children sequestered themselves in Makuzu-an, a small sub-temple of Chion-in. According to one account, Rengetsu was pregnant at the time of Hisatoshi's death and a few months later gave birth to a son named Jomu. At Makuzu-an, Rengetsu cared for her children and aging father. Rengetsu and her father spent hours chanting the *nembutsu*. They also resumed playing high-level *go* as one of their few consolations. In 1825, Rengetsu's daughter Chigyoku died at the age of seven. In 1827, her son Jomu died at age five.[3] In August of 1832, Rengetsu's father—a man who had lost his wife, all five sons, two adopted sons, and all his grandchildren—died at age 78. At age 42, Rengetsu was alone.

---

[3] There has always been the question, "How many children did Rengetsu actually have?" Late in life, Rengetsu herself wrote, "I lost two daughters and one son," perhaps meaning two daughters and a son that lived for more than a year because there is solid evidence that she lost four, most likely five children as described above. Tomioka Tessai, who knew more about Rengetsu than anyone, stated that "Six of her children died." There is a slight possibility that Tayuinosho Senri (1814–1896) was her son, although it is recorded that Senri was her nephew. Senri was a well-known scholar, agitator (he was imprisoned for a time by the Bakufu), advocate of Western military science, adventurer, and pioneer. Rengetsu kept in close touch with Senri all her life, and from the nature of her letters to Senri, she clearly loved him like a son, but it may be that she "adopted" him because all her other children were dead.

THE MIDDLE YEARS

After the 49-day mourning period for her father had passed, Rengetsu left Makuzu-an. She held no official position at Chion-in. There were few Buddhist nuns in Japan, no nunnery to speak of, and the abbesses at the temples typically were members of the imperial household and had taken vows late in life to serve at a temple sponsored by the emperor. And while there were some mendicant monks who survived by begging, that was not an option for a solitary nun. Rengetsu had no place within a Buddhist organization.

Thus, she needed a livelihood—perhaps as a martial arts instructor, but it took money and official support from a samurai domain to open a *dojo.* Since Rengetsu had been playing *go* from the time she was a little girl, she was talented. She had attracted mostly male students who were much more interested in her beauty than in her skill. Rengetsu realized that it would be difficult to have male students take her seriously. Further, Rengetsu was not yet accomplished enough to attract poetry or calligraphy students.

After Rengetsu moved to the Okazaki district of Kyoto, she wrote in her autobiography that pottery making was the answer to the problem of making a living. However, there were dozens of kilns in Kyoto selling high-quality ceramics based on centuries of craftsmanship. Rengetsu only learned the rudiments of pottery making—all her training was informal, which had probably consisted of trying her hand at pottery making when she was living at Makuzu-an and later learning from an amateur grandma potter in the Awata kiln district—so she could not compete on a technical level. However, Rengetsu thought that if she incised her original poems in a pleasing manner on inexpensive pottery that would attract customers. She wrote in her autobiography: "My pottery was poorly crafted and unskillfully made, but I did my best to make each piece unique." Rengetsu's first efforts were simple things such as small teapots and cups made for the *sencha* tea ceremony, flower vases, sake cups, plates, and the like. She composed this poem entitled "Forming a Flower Vase out of Clay:"

> Taking my amateur,
> Rough little things
> To sell—
> How forlorn they look
> In the market place!

However, since Rengetsu's unadorned, unpretentious pottery actually stood out among all the other highly polished and colorful professional pieces, Rengetsu-yaki was a big hit,[4] and pottery making turned out to be Rengetsu's primary means of support for the rest of her life.

The entire period of Rengetsu's life from her midforties to her mid-fifties is a mystery. Although Rengetsu lived frugally, it is difficult to believe that initially she earned enough money from pottery making to survive. There is speculation that during this time, she received financial support from the extended Otagaki family or other patrons.

---

[4] Rengetsu-yaki is the name applied to pottery made by Rengetsu herself and with the cooperation of helpers in her workshop.

Since Rengetsu was uncommonly beautiful—a widespread rumor in Kyoto was that she had once been a courtesan in the pleasure quarters—she was constantly being accosted by men, even after she became a nun. The story goes that Rengetsu went so far as to pull out her front teeth to make herself less attractive. Even that did not work. Rengetsu continued to be widely known as the "beautiful nun in Kyoto" throughout her life. Nomura Boto (1806–1867) wrote about a visit to Rengetsu: "I heard that she was in her mid-seventies but she looked 50. She is still very attractive, even as a nun. She must have been a stunning beauty when she was young."

Early in her middle years, Rengetsu learned to paint. According to several accounts, Rengetsu was the student and live-in lover of the *Shijo* painter Matsumura Keibun (1779–1843). It may seem surprising for a nun to have a love affair, but in Japan, the vow of celibacy was never taken seriously—in the Jodo Shinshu sect, priests have been openly marrying since the 13ᵗʰ century.

Rengetsu had close contact with other *Shijo* painters such as Nakajima Raisho (1796–1871), Yokoyama Seiki (1792–1864), Kishi Renzan (1804–1859), Mori Kansai (1814–1894), and Shiokawa

Bunrin (1808–1877). At one time or another, Rengetsu did joint works with all these artists. She also did a number of joint works with Reizei Tamechika (1823–1864), who was one of the revivers of the Yamato-e style of painting.[5]

Regarding poetry composition, Rengetsu wrote, "I did not have the leisure to study poetry composition at length, nor could I find a good teacher that I liked." Naturally, Rengetsu had learned the basics of poetry composition from her father and during her service at the castle, but she did not study the art in depth at any particular school. Rengetsu read widely in classical and modern poetry, and she wrote that she was influenced by the theories of such poets as Ozawa Roan (1723–1801), Kagawa Kageki (1768–1843), and later by the Shinto priest, nationalist scholar, and poet Mutobe Yoshika (1798–1864). However, her poetry cannot be characterized as belonging to any one tradition.

As for Rengetsu's brushwork, there are examples of her calligraphy dating from her forties. Although her calligraphy was nothing special then, Rengetsu

[5] The relationship between Rengetsu, Keibun, and the Shijo school of painting is discussed in the Japanese publication *Otagaki Rengetsu* by Sugimoto Hidetaro, pp. 132–136. As is the case with all the arts she studied, Rengetsu developed her own style of painting, so it is impossible to place her firmly in one school or the other.

developed a distinctive and remarkably original brushwork; it does not show the influence of any previous style. There is nothing like it. A primary reason why Rengetsu acquired such a strong steady hand in her brushwork is that from the beginning, she was incising her poems in wet clay. That requires extraordinary strength and perfect placement. The characters have to be clean and legible. In short, during this middle period, Rengetsu learned to make and market pottery, refined her calligraphy, learned how to paint, studied poetry in various styles, and established contacts with many of the artists, literary figures, scholars, and political activists of the day.

FULFILLMENT

Rengetsu hit her stride at age 60 and went on to produce a huge corpus of work—poetry, calligraphy, pottery, painting, and collaborations—over the next 25 years.

In 1851 at age 61, Rengetsu took a break from her pottery making to spend the summer in retreat at Daibutsu (Hoko-ji), mostly to study the collected poetry of Ozawa Roan. The head priest at a nearby temple, Myoho-in, was Rakei Jihon (1795–1868). Jihon was a Tendai Buddhist savant as well as a poet and calligrapher. Rengetsu and Jihon became good friends. While at Daibutsu, Rengetsu also met Gankai Ajari (1823–1874), who was another

prominent Tendai scholar and marathon monk
from Mt. Hiei. Rengetsu gave Gankai a teapot that
he treasured the rest of his days. We can surmise
that Rengetsu acquired a good knowledge of Tendai
Buddhism when she was at Daibutsu, regularly
attending the morning service or other ceremonies at
the temple and talking with Jihon and Gankai.

After her time at Daibutsu, Rengetsu seems to have
lived in or around Okazaki until 1856. At age 66,
Rengetsu moved to Shinsho-ji, a recently restored
Soto Shu Zen temple in the Kita-Shirakawa area,
at the invitation of the new head priest Hara Tanzan
(1819–1892). Young Tomioka Tessai, who had
become Rengetsu's protégé a few years earlier, moved
there as well to look after her and help out with the
pottery making.[6] Eccentric Tanzan was one of the
zaniest Zen masters of the day. Tanzan has been
immortalized in modern Zen lore as the hero of this
oft repeated tale:

[6] Tomioka Tessai (1837–1924), later to become the last great literati artist of
modern times, began lodging with Rengetsu in his early twenties. Rengetsu
became his mentor, patron, and mother figure who treated him like a son.
Tessai helped Rengetsu with her pottery making, and later she repaid the favor by
inscribing her poems on the unknown young artist Tessai's paintings so they would
sell better. Like any mother, Rengetsu pestered the single Tessai to marry when he
was in his early 30s. Rengetsu and Tessai continued to create joint works up to the
very end of Rengetsu's life.

Two novice monks, Tanzan and Ekido, were on a pilgrimage from one training monastery to another. A storm blew up, and the pair came to a flooded crossroad that had been transformed into a fast-flowing stream. A lovely young girl was stranded there. Tanzan inquired, "Do you need help?" When the girl replied, "Yes," he lifted her up on his shoulders, carried her across the flooded road, and deposited her safely on the other side. After the two monks walked a bit farther, Ekido burst out, "How could you do such a thing? You know it is strictly prohibited for Buddhist monks to touch women!" (And on top of that, in those days, Japanese women did not use underwear.) Tanzan shot back, "What? Are you still carrying that girl? I put her down long ago."

Rengetsu spent hours discussing Zen Buddhism with Tanzan, and most probably took part in some of Shinsho-ji's temple activities including Zen meditation.

Rengetsu lived at Shinsho-ji for a couple of years and then moved to Shogo-in village. She lived in Shogo-in until 1863, and at age 73, she moved to Nishigamo, where she lived in a hut near the farm family of Yoshida Yasu. (Yasu assisted Rengetsu with pottery making.)

Finally in 1865, Rengetsu settled down. After leaving Chion-in, Rengetsu had moved her residence more than 30 times—13 moves in one year—and she was nicknamed "Always on the Move Rengetsu." (She kept all her possessions in a small box that allowed her to move on an instant's notice.) At age 75, Rengetsu moved permanently into the tea hut at Jinko-in.

According to legend, Kobo Daishi, the founder of Shingon Buddhism in Japan, engaged in ascetic practices for 90 days on the spot where the temple now stands. In 1217, a Shinto priest at Kamigamo Shrine named Matsushita Norihisa saw a divine light shining on the mountain. He arranged to have a temple constructed there he called Jinko ("Divine Light"). Over the centuries Jinko-in became a center of Shingon Buddhism. Worship at Jinko-in was said to be especially efficacious for those suffering from eye-disease. The iris pond and the crimson maple leaves on the grounds of Jinko-in are famed for their beauty.

The head priest at Jinko-in was Wada Gesshin (1800–1870). Gesshin was originally a professional painter under the name Gozan. At age 42 after the death of his wife, Gozan, with two of his sons, took ordination as a Shingon Buddhist monk. He took the religious name Gesshin, "Moon Mind." While Gesshin remained an artist, primarily as a painter of Buddha, Kannon, and Jizo images, his sons Kakuju ("Bodhi Tree") and Chiman ("Full of Knowledge") become important and influential figures in the history of modern Buddhism.

Chiman (1836–1910) was living with his father at Jinko-in and was Rengetsu's preceptor. She became a serious practitioner of Tantric Buddhism. In Rengetsu's tea hut, an image of Fudo Myo-o, patron saint of esoteric Buddhists, was placed in the alcove. She chanted Tantric mantra throughout the day.

Gesshin and Rengetsu became close collaborators as artists, Gesshin doing the painting and Rengetsu adding the poetic inscription. Their joint pieces were not limited to religious subjects; their art covered the entire range of human affairs, historical events, and the world of nature. The pair produced many fine pieces.

At Jinko-in, Rengetsu continued to make pottery, brush calligraphy, paint, and collaborate with many other artists. For years, Rengetsu had been complaining of various ailments and lamenting how old and frail she was becoming.

She wrote the poem "Upon Turning Age 77:"

> Another year has arrived—
> If I die, it is fine,
> If I live, it is fine.
> It is fine all the same.
> I may go but spring comes once again.[7]

In fact, Rengetsu's 77th year was by far the most productive and vital period of her life. Thousands of pieces in all media—clay, paper, and wood—are proudly signed, "Rengetsu, age 77." During her late years, Rengetsu's calligraphy with brush on paper or with pick in clay is extraordinarily bold, powerful, and confident.

During her eighties, Rengetsu did slow down a bit, but as she became weaker physically, her work became stronger, particularly her tea bowls. Her tea bowls were made more slowly, with gravitas, and a deeper sense of *wabi* and *sabi*. Rengetsu began doing more albums containing her own work and collaborations with other artists (mostly Tessai) and also compiled many sketchbooks.

---

[7] Rengetsu's state of mind was based on her bitter experience of the transient nature of life rather than the actual condition of her health. Despite her grumbling, judging from the huge output of work Rengetsu produced in her 70s and 80s, she remained robust until the last couple of months of her life.

Although Rengetsu had no intention of publishing a collection of her poetry—and in fact opposed it—her friends were insistent. In 1868, when Rengetsu was 78, *Rengetsu Shikibu nijo waka shu* (*Poems by Rengetsu and Shikibu*) was published. Takabatake Shikibu (1785–1881) was Rengetsu's fellow poet and artist; they also collaborated on paintings. This collection had 50 poems by Shikibu and 49 by Rengetsu. In 1870, *Ama no Karumo* (*A Diver's Harvest of Seaweed*) was published. This edition had 310 poems by Rengetsu alone. All in all, there are around 900 extant *waka* collected in various editions of Rengetsu's poetry, and variations and new poems continue to be discovered.

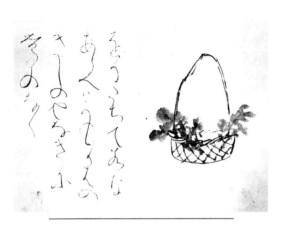

FINAL DAYS

When Rengetsu was 84, Tessai asked her to write an autobiography. It turned out two pages long. Rengetsu did not write much more than "I was born in Kyoto, as I child I was called Nobu, I lost my family, I became a nun in my thirties, I made pottery to support myself, and I am now old and frail."

The biography consists primarily of poems. After mentioning that she has lost all her loved ones, Rengetsu gives these two poems:

> The evanescence of
> This floating world
> I feel over and over:
> It is hardest to be
> The one left behind.

Often I recall the love
Of my father
When I visit his grave,
I can only
Sob and sob.

She goes on, adding these poems:

I have abandoned this
World of dreams,
But in my dreams
I cannot settle down
Thinking about these times of trouble.

This dew-like body,
So fleeting—
[My life has been like]
A weather-beaten grass hut lying
In the shade of a mountain.

At day break,
I am off to gather clay
To make my pottery;
It is my way of
Venerating Buddha.

Her biography ends with the farewell poem "Gazing Upon the Sky at Sunset:"

> No more grime
> Left in my heart;
> All there is—
> Today's cloudless sky
> At sunset.

In October of 1875, Rengetsu fell sick with typhoid fever. Near the end, Rengetsu spent most of her time in meditation, chanting the *nembutsu*, and reciting mantras. When people brought her medicine, she told them kindly, "My time has come. No need to waste medicine on me."

Rengetsu continued creating art to the very end. Her final work of art, an album of her inscriptions on Tessai's paintings, was finished a couple of days before her death. Rengetsu's final letter was composed three days prior to her passing. Head Priest Chiman was sequestered in the main hall of Jinko-in, fasting and praying for Rengetsu's recovery. She thanked Chiman for his efforts but told him that her life was now at an end: "This is my last letter." In her final days, Rengetsu was lovingly cared for by her closest disciple, the nun Mokujaku.

Rengetsu died in her tea hut at Jinko-in on December 10th. She requested that her death be kept quiet with only Tessai to be informed. After Tessai arrived, her body was wrapped in a white shroud and the weeping villagers carried Rengetsu's coffin up the hill to her grave site at Saiho-ji. Rengetsu's grave site is marked by a small simple stone tucked away in a corner of the cemetery next to a huge cherry tree.

Gravestone of Otagaki Rengetsu. The calligraphy, "Otagaki Rengetsu Tomb" was brushed by Tomioka Tessai. (Photograph by Andy Kay.)

Poetry of
LOTUS MOON

PREFACE TO THE FIRST COLLECTION
OF RENGETSU'S POETRY

There is a nun who passes her days quietly, living at the base of Mount Hiei, surrounded by greenery. The flowing waters of the Kamo River cleanse her heart. She digs clay from the riverbank, mixes it with water, and creates many kinds of pottery that she sells to support herself. She also loves poetry. The nun's name is Rengetsu, "Lotus Moon." People clamor to buy her simple, unadorned pottery and to request elegant calligraphy of her poetry. Although she remains in the shadows, so many people come to visit her that she feels compelled to move to more and more remote places.

The number of poems collected here is not as large as one would expect. She has composed a large number of poems, many of which are incised on her pottery, but the ones collected here are the most beloved.

I recall the days long ago when Rengetsu appeared in the capital, clad in her black robes and with a serene countenance. I did not want the memory of her work to fade away, so I visited her at her little hut hidden in Saga to discuss an edition of her poems. She was decrepit, skin and bones, bent at the hips, but her face remained radiant. She had grown very old, having spent more than 40 years, creating beautiful things. Her life had been full. It is my hope that the publication of this collection will enable many more people to come to know and love Rengetsu's poetry.

—Fujiwara Toju, February 1st, 1872
for the first edition of *Ama no Karumo*

SPRING

MOUNTAIN RETREAT[1]

Living deep in the mountain
I have grown fond of the
Sound of murmuring pines;
On days the wind does not blow,
How lonely it is!

---

[1] "Mountain Retreat" is not, strictly speaking, a spring poem. During Rengetsu's lifetime, this was her most well-known piece, often recited at parties and social gatherings during all seasons.

SPRING MOON

In the moonlight
Of early spring,
Lingering snow
Bids farewell to a village
Yearning for its first flower.

TENDER BUDS

A thousand grasses
Run rampant in autumn
But to discover a
Single sprout with two buds:
The joy of spring!

SPRING ICE

The thick river ice
Begins to break,
The mountain well
Starts to thaw
Allowing me to scoop up spring.

SPRING SUNRISE

Dawn today—
High above the river,
Mountains thickset with snow;
Down below,
The roar of flowing water.

UPON HEARING THE FIRST UGUISU OF SPRING[2]

Amid the plum blossoms,
The first burst of song;
Too young to give a
Full-throated performance,
So we have to smile.

---

[2] In Japanese art and poetry, an *uguisu* (Japanese nightingale) is always paired with plum blossoms. A plum tree, the first plant to flower in the spring, is a symbol of endurance and renewal; the *uguisu*, a tiny bird of great beauty, breaks into song at the coming of the new season. *Uguisu* do not chirp but sing. The bird's cry sounds like *Hokke-kyo*, the Japanese title of the *Lotus Sutra*.

PLUM BLOSSOMS

Eagerly awaiting
The uguisu:
The lovely plum blossoms
Along my garden wall
Burst into bloom.

A DAY THE PLUM TREES
NEAR MY HERMITAGE
WERE IN BLOOM

When the uguisu
Come to the capital
I'd like to lend them
My little hut—
Plum blossoms are waiting.

EVENING PLUM BLOSSOMS

As the night advances
The fragrance of the blossoms
Perfumes both the
Sleeves of my black robe
And the recesses of my heart.

PLUM BLOSSOMS
NORTH AND SOUTH

Morning moon:
At my door,
Fragrant blossoms
Right and left—
Please linger a little longer.

RETURNING GEESE

Flocks of returning geese,
But I cannot see
Where they are heading
In the evening mist—
Nothing but the trace of their cries.

This world of ours
Is as fleeting as geese
Flying across the sky—
Such sad thoughts
Make my tears fall like rain.

SPRING WIND

Spring wind
Come once again—
Do not be too rough
On the delicate branches and buds
Of the weeping willows.

SPRING DRIZZLE
IN THE MORNING

No sound,
Can't see it:
The morning drizzle
Weighs lightly
On the green willow branches.

WILLOWS
IN AN ANCIENT VILLAGE

It looks like a cloud of smoke
But as I come closer
To the old house
In this ancient village
I see it is a billowing willow.

THE WILLOW AT THE WINDOW

So quickly!
The willow
Planted three years ago
Now beating against
My windowpane.

VIOLETS

In Kasuga Field
That ancient place,
Little purple violets
Gather again
Like old friends

HINAMATSURI[3]

As an offering today to
The lord and lady dolls
Freshly opened peach blossoms—
The joy of countless springs
Is once again ours.

---

[3] On the Third Day of the Third Month there is Hinamatsuri, the Doll Festival. In nearly every home, a pair of dolls representing the emperor and empress (and symbolic of all couples) is displayed on a shelf. Peach blossoms appear in full bloom around the same time of the year, making the occasion doubly festive.

MIST

From morning,
Perfectly tranquil,
Far removed from
The world's turmoil—
I am one with the spring mist.

UPON HEARING THE BELL AT YOSHIMIZU[4]

The echo of the temple bell
At Yoshimizu—
I am here, too,
In a black robe
Set against the white mist.

---

[4] Yoshimizu is a spot in Kyoto's Higashiyama district noted for its beautiful scenery and temples. The large temple bell is struck once early in the morning and once in the evening. The sound of the bell reverberates throughout the hills.

WAITING FOR THE CHERRY BLOSSOMS

Too early for cherry blossoms
So I must wait in my
Ramshackle hut beneath the trees,
Sipping sake
As cold spring rain falls.

BLOSSOMS ON ARASHIYAMA[5]

Feeling reborn,
My heart renewed.
Freed from the world of sorrow,
By the sight of blossoms at daybreak
On Arashiyama.

---

[5] Arashiyama, a district in Kyoto, means "Stormy Mountain." There is a play on words suggesting that "During the raging storms of life, you are still able to find a beautiful place of repose, both without and within."

BLOSSOMS

So many bright
Cherry blossoms
All around—
I cannot decide if they resemble
Billowing clouds or flakes of snow.

Even though I will
Come tomorrow
I'll take a branch of
Mountain blossoms
To keep me company.

A TRIP DURING
CHERRY BLOSSOM SEASON

No place for me at the inn
But I find consolation
Sleeping beneath the
Hazy moon and the
Cherry blossoms.

BLOSSOMS AT NONOMIYA SHRINE[6]

Within the imperial shrine
That shelters princesses
Spring purification rites are made;
At the gate, cherry blossoms
Amid the sakaki leaves.

LATE SPRING BLOSSOMS

Late spring, I wonder if
I am too late;
No, I am relieved to see
That splendid cherry blossoms
Still linger on the mountains of Oshiho.[7]

---

[6] Nonomiya in Kyoto is an imperial shrine where a princess secludes herself for a year to perform purification rites. The cherry blossoms are the Buddhist flower of impermanence; the sakaki is the scared tree of Shinto.

[7] Oshiho is the area surrounding Saiko-ji in Nara. It is famous for the "one thousand cherry trees that bloom in spring."

SCATTERED BLOSSOMS

Cherry blossoms
Scatter at the peak of their beauty—
It is much harder for us
To fall away from our own
Attachment to the world.

The flowers
Bloom and quickly fall
In quiet splendor
Blessing us with
Their brief presence.

THE BUTTERFLY[8]

Fluttering
In a field of
Flowers and dew—
In whose dream
Is this butterfly?

---

[8] This refers to the famous dream of Zhuangzi: "Am I a man dreaming I am a butterfly or a butterfly dreaming I am a man?"

SUMMER

EARLY SUMMER

The blossoms have fallen,
The fetters of my heart
Have been loosened,
And it has become summer:
A stream murmurs cold and clear.

EARLY SUMMER BREEZE

Abundant clouds,
Flowers reaching full bloom,
Fresh summer mountains,
Fragrant green leaves
And gentle cool breezes.

UNOHANA[1]

Unohana shrubs
Form a living fence
That shuts out worldly cares—
Even the name of the flower
Sounds delightful.

---

[1] Unohana (*deutzia crenta*) is a shrub with small white flowers that bloom in early summer. The shrubs are often planted around a dwelling to form a hedge.

FIRST CRY OF THE HOTOTOGISU[2]

When will it sing?
In this ancient village
The hototogisu
Conceals itself
Until the fourth month.

WAITING FOR THE CALL
OF A HOTOTOGISU

Waiting for the
The call of a
Hototogisu
In the white light
Of the morning moon.

---

[2] *Hototogisu* is the Japanese cuckoo. Similar to the *uguisu,* the cry of a *hototogisu* marks the beginning of a new season, in this case summer. The call of a *hototogisu* at daybreak is considered especially beautiful.

IN THE VICINITY OF MT. KASE

Still light—
The hototogisu's song
Here at my hut on Mt. Kase
Will be my souvenir tomorrow
When I make my way to the capital.

THE HORSE RACES AT KAMO ON THE FIFTH DAY OF THE FIFTH MONTH[3]

"Do not fall behind,
Run, run faster!"
[We yell for our favorite horse]:
Even the hototogisu on Kamiyama
Seem to join in the cheer.

---

[3] The Fifth Day of the Fifth Month is Tango no Sekku, the day marking the official start of the summer festival season, as well as Boys' Day. On that day, horse races are held on the grounds of Kamo Shrine (referred to as Kamiyama in the poem). The event is one of the highlights of the summer season.

FIFTH DAY OF
THE FIFTH MONTH[4]

Already abundant
Butterbur
Mix with the iris
and mugwort
Surrounding my hut.

---

[4] On this day as well, irises (called *hanashobu*, "flower of victory") are festooned everywhere. Butterbur (*fuki*) is another early summer flower; *fuki* can also mean "riches" and a "person of noble character" so the two flowers are paired as good luck charms for boys. Sometimes irises and mugwort (*yomogi*) are hung together outside of a house. The strong medicinal smell of mugwort is believed to repel evil spirits. Rengetsu had the good fortune to have many such plants and flowers in her garden.

LISTENING TO A HOTOTOGISU CALL OVER AND OVER

I have borne a grudge
For too long—
Today, in a thick grove
A hototogisu called out to me
Over and over to let it go.

KUKINA[5]

In the faint moonlight
Barely visible
A thin wooden bridge:
Underneath water flows away
While waterfowl cry.

---

[5] The cry of a *kukina*, a kind of waterfowl that lives in marshes, sounds like *knock, knock*. In English as well as Japanese, *knock, knock* connotes that someone has arrived. There is a contrast between the water flowing away and the waterfowl arriving.

ANCIENT VILLA FLOWERS

The single memento of
A once great family:
Little sunflowers
Along the fence
Of the abandoned villa.

EVENING COOL BY THE SEA

Cooling off in boat
That sways as if drunk—
In the bay breeze
The moon on the waves
Seems a bit tipsy too!

MOON IN THE SUMMER TREES

What a delight—
Leaves shade my little hut
From the hot sun by day
But let the moonlight
Filter through at night.

SUMMER MOON

The cool shadow
Of the bright moon
In an open field
Makes you forget
All daytime worries.

A HERMIT'S MOON

All alone inside
Nothing outside
But moonbeams
Come to visit
My tumbledown hut.

MOSQUITO SMUDGE

Seaside village:
Mosquito smudge molders
Throughout the cool evening,
But the thin smoke leaves
The moon untouched.

SUMMER TRAVEL

Such heat on this journey—
The young girls
Working at their looms in this village
Need to take off
And have a long nap.

BAMBOO

This noble gentleman
Adds node after node
Auspiciously:
Learn from it and
You will ever flourish.

CORMORANT RIVER FIREFLIES[6]

The flittering fireflies
Willingly sacrifice
Themselves
To the torches
On the Cormorant River.

---

[6] Cormorants—bound around the neck to prevent them swallowing the fish—were used to catch river fish at night. The fish are attracted to the torches hung from the boats.

LOTUS

No dew yet
So no place for the moon to settle,
Yet still lovely—
The surface of my garden pond
Covered with lotus blossoms.

If I too could somehow
Open the lotus blossom
Within my own heart
And color it pure white
How happy I would be. . . .

INSCRIPTION ON PAINTING
OF EGGPLANTS

In this floating world
Things that mature well
Produce happy thoughts.
Eggplants becoming ripe[7]
Is a matter of great celebration.

---

[7] Mission accomplished.

BATS IN THE MOONLIGHT

In the pale moonlight,
Near the eaves of my hut,
Bats fluttering about the
Swaying willow branches,
Bring back fond memories.

CICADAS

No light yet,
Night lingers on,
But already from the tops
Of the trees hiding my hut
Cicadas shriek.

RAINY SEASON[8]

A steady sprinkle,
No sight of the sun,
Day after day,
Forests swallowed by clouds:
Rainy season.

Pouring all night,
The storm kept me awake;
Not only that,
I cannot kindle the firewood
Soaked with rain.

---

[8] In Japan, the monsoon season runs from late May through June. It is a period of constant clouds and frequent rain, typically heavy and seemingly unending.

MOONFLOWERS

The silver crescent
Shines dimly
But the night is
Brightened by
The moonflowers.

NADESHIKO[9]

Gazing at the nadeshiko
Flowers covered with dew
Makes me recall how I once smoothed out
My children's tangled
Morning hair on my sleeve.

---

[9] *Nadeshiko* is a shrub with light pink flowers that bloom from late spring to early autumn. In poetry, the flower is associated with tenderness, purity, love, and beauty.

TACHIBANA[10]

As I gather
Tachibana blossoms
I get lost in thought—
No, no need for that,
Enjoy the moment at hand.

[10] *Tachibana* is a green citrus tree. The fruit is inedible but the blossoms have a good smell. In poetry, *tachibana* are associated with poignant thoughts of lost loved ones.

AUTUMN

THE BEGINNING OF AUTUMN

In the morning breeze
Willows along the riverbank
Start to drop their leaves
Into the flowing water—
Autumn is arriving. . . .

AUTUMN RETREAT

Deep in the mountains
A single branch of crimson leaves
Near the eves of my hut
Marks the beginning
Of the days of autumn.

AUTUMN FROST

Just starting to
Form along the
The base of the mountains
The thin mist
Has yet to enter Akishino Village.[1]

---

[1] Akishino is a district in Nara famous for the mist that settles there in autumn.

ENJOYING AN AUTUMN EVENING

In the fields, in the mountains
I was enthralled, so enthralled—
The autumn moon
Accompanied me
Right to my bedroom.

AN IMMORTAL'S ELIXIR[2]

Chrysanthemum dew;
Lift it up.
Take a big sip
And you will be immortal,
Not aging, not dying!

---

[2] Daoist immortals are said to maintain their longevity by "feasting on dew."

MUMBLING TO MYSELF ON THE NINTH DAY OF THE NINTH MONTH[3]

Picking chrysanthemums,
Hoping to recapture my youth:
My old body, however, has piled up
More years than this
Growing mound of flowers!

---

[3] The Ninth Day of the Ninth Month is considered the peak of the chrysanthemum season, and an ancient Chinese legend has it that if one gathers flowers on this day and prepares a concoction of the petals, one's life will be greatly lengthened.

GAZING AT THE MOON
NIGHT AFTER NIGHT[4]

The autumn moon—
It, too,
Can become
A tie to the
Floating world.

---

[4] The autumn moon, a symbol of enlightenment, is an object of contemplation for Buddhists.

AS A NUN, GAZING AT THE DEEP COLORS OF AUTUMN

Clad in black robes,
I should have no attachments to
The shapes and scents of this world
But how can I keep my vows
Gazing on today's crimson maple leaves?

A VISIT TO TAGANO-O TO VIEW THE CRIMSON MAPLE LEAVES

I cannot leave without
Breaking off a branch of
Tagano-o maple leaves—
If a few leaves happen to fall
Please forgive me, mountain guardians.

LIVING NEXT TO
THE GREAT BUDDHA

My nights:
Autumn chill,
A steady drizzle
Of cold rain, and
The flicker of lonely shadows.

CHESTNUTS

Amid the
Crimson leaves
Mountain chestnuts
Ripe with burrs:
The blessings of autumn.

I know it is naughty for a nun,
But I ask the girls
Gathering chestnuts
To fetch me some sake
From the village.

MOUNTAIN VILLAGE FOG

Overgrown with kudzu vines,
Not a visitor for ages;
Along the hedge
Autumn fog wells up
In this mountain village.

FIELD OF WILD GRASSES

Rather than cutting them down
To spread out or gather up,
Let the wild grasses of autumn be—
I want to enjoy the field
Just as it is. . . .

Not wanting the grasses
To flower
Nor even to seed—
I gaze at the autumn fields
Stretching on and on.

AUTUMN RAIN

The sun sets
And the shadows deepen
Around the pines of Irie[5]—
Lonely memories
In the autumn rain.

---

[5] Irie is the old name for the area around Chion-in—Rengetsu's home temple.

SEASHORE MOON

I walk along Akashi Bay[6]
This moonlit autumn evening
Trying to pick up
Words beautiful enough
To capture the scene.

---

[6] Akashi Bay is one of Japan's famed scenic spots for moon viewing.

In autumn I visited a mountain temple. The wild bush clover mingled with the flowering pampas grass along the hedge, and various insects sang in unison. When the moment captivates you . . .

> Perfectly aware
> Not a thought,
> Just the moon
> Piercing me with light.
> As I gaze upon it.

PURE MOONLIGHT

Across the ancient fields
Bunches of moss
Mingle with thick grass;
My heart, too, is brightened
The pure moonlight.

Living in the mountains
I have grown old,
No longer needing much sleep—
I am always up at dawn
To greet the morning moon.

INSECTS CHIRPING
IN THE MOONLIGHT

From a crack in the wall
Of my mountain hut:
Katydids announce themselves;
Moonlight too
Pours in.

In the pure moonlight
A chorus of insects
Chirp along the hedge:
The cold, too, deepens
As the night lengthens.

THE CRY OF INSECTS DURING A TRIP

The moon is bright,
The insects sing;
I put up in a makeshift grass hut
Drifting off to sleep
A single sleeve for my pillow.

AUTUMN TEARS

In the sky,
Flocks of departing geese;
In the weeds,
Murmuring insects—
Tears like dew well up in my eyes.

AT A SHRINE

Autumn chorus:
Wind in the pines,
Bell cricket melodies
At a country shrine
Decorated with sacred festoons.

THE PLEASURES OF
AN AUTUMN EVENING

On each dew drop,
I count one
Moon after another,
All night
Until daybreak.

AUTUMN PADDIES

Pouring rain,
Evening gloom,
In the mountain paddies:
Other than a scarecrow,
Not a soul around.

FOG IN THE FIELDS

Making my way
Through the fog on
The road to Oyama[7]—
The only person I saw
Turned out to be a scarecrow.

---

[7] Oyama is a district in central Kyoto.

POUNDING CLOTH[8]

For those pounding cloth
It is a way to pound out
The grime in their hearts;
The moon grows brighter and brighter
As the villagers pound away.

The night deepens
As I pound and pound out
The dirt and grime from
My threadbare nun's robe
Here in Shino Village.

---

[8] In the cool, clear air of autumn, kimono were pounded at night to remove the dirt and improve the gloss.

CHRYSANTHEMUMS

White chrysanthemums
Near my pillow
Scent the night;
My fleeting dreams, too,
Fade away with autumn.

INVITATION

People from the capital
Please come up to Okazaki
To see the moon;
I will cook yams for you
Taken from my garden.

WINTER

FIRST WINTER RAIN

Still crimson,
In the shade of maple leaves,
I take shelter:
Somehow I am happy
To feel the first rain of winter.

FIRST WINTER FROST

Yes, autumn is
Really gone:
Dew has now
Become hard frost
Around my hut.

As the moon ascends
Plovers cry in the shoals
Along the Kamo River bank[1]—
Night deepens, first frost
Settles on my sleeves.

---

[1] Kamogawa-tsutsumi is a path that runs along the Kamo River. It is famous for its beauty: cherry blossoms in spring and colorful foliage in autumn. In art, the Kamo River shoals and the plovers are frequently paired. This poem was written in the tenth month when the moon is changing from an autumn moon to a winter moon.

EARLY WINTER

On the top branches
A few persimmons
Have yet to fall—
So the colors of autumn
Linger in my sight.

SCATTERED LEAVES

The fierce mountain wind
Has scattered all the remaining leaves;
Above the wall of
An ancient temple
The sun sets faintly.

MOUNTAIN RETREAT
IN WINTER

The little persimmons drying outside
Under the eaves
Of my hermitage—
Are they freezing tonight
In the winter storm?

FALLEN LEAVES
AROUND MY HUT

A pile of fallen leaves
As high as a mountain
Separates my hermitage
Further and further
From the world of woe.

WINTER CONFINEMENT IN
SHIGARAKI VILLAGE

Last night's storm was fierce,
As I can see by this morning's
Thick blanket of snow:
I rise to kindle wood chips,
In lonely Shigaraki Village.[2]

---

[2] Rengetsu often stayed in Shigaraki Village to dig clay for her pottery.

FROZEN LAKE

The freezing wind
Along the shore
Has frozen the lake:
The ferry boats have
Been captured by ice.

A DAY OF SLEET

Will the paper on the
Makeshift
Little window of my hut
Withstand the assault
Of sleet?

STORM

The pine branches
That provide my shade
Are driven down
Against my window
By the raging snowstorm.

SEASHORE SNOW

The sea breeze
Gradually calms
As the night lengthens
And lustrous white snow
Piles up on the pines of Naruo.[3]

---

[3] The seashore at Naruo is noted for its splendid pines.

SNOWFALL OVER A RIVER

The river wind
Blows frothy snow
All about—
But it does not appear to
Settle anywhere on the water.

COLD NIGHT

The frigid north wind
Blows through the spaces of
My tattered window screen;
The cold blast keeps both the screen
And my eyes open all night.

KAGURA IN THE VILLAGE[4]

The beating of a drum
 Keeping the hours
Mixes with the sacred music:
The moon is good, the kagura splendid
Here in Yoshida Village.

The pervasive sound of bells
Coming from the evening kagura
Makes me envious of the
Performers engulfed
By the music.

---

[4] Hours were announced by a timekeeper beating a large drum. *Kagura* is sacred
music and dancing performed at a Shinto shrine. *Yoshida* means "good field."

WINTER DREAMS

To forget the chill of
The frozen hearth
I spend the night
Dreaming of gathering
Violets on spring fields.

ICE IN THE MOUNTAIN WELL

Yesterday,
I shattered the ice
To draw water—
No matter, this morning the water
Froze just as solid.

YEAR END

Time has flown by,
In this field of dreams;
Night by night
The frost lightens
As the year comes to an end.

YEAR END MOON

Looking back on the year,
I made it through
But I grew one year more decrepit;
The twelfth month draws to a close
Under the half-moon.

OLD AGE IN THE NEW YEAR

I count off the days remaining
Until spring arrives
But I know that
I will greet the New Year
A little more stooped.

REMOVING THE SOOT

Clearing out
The dust and grime
In my heart as well
I try to make everything spotless
At the end of the year.

MISCELLANEOUS

ALONG THE UJI RIVER RECALLING THE PAST[1]

Here the brave warriors
Of old once
Forded these shallows—
Now their names borne away
By the water of Uji River.

---

[1] The shallows near Uji Bridge were the site of several famous battles between the Minamoto and Taira clans during the 12th century.

RIVER

The floating world's
Dust and dirt
Flows away
And all is purified
By the waves of Kamo River.[2]

---

[2] Kamo River runs through the center of Kyoto.

LIVING BY A RIVER

Living along the river
The pure water,
Day after day
Seems to wash away
My sins and faults.

In this world of ours
As we cross from shore to shore[3]
We should keep our thoughts
As unsullied as
Flowing water.

---

[3] "Cross from shore to shore" refers to the Buddhist notion of crossing from the shore of illusion to the far shore of enlightenment.

THOUGHTS

If only we could
Cut down the weeds
In our hearts
As cleanly as the razor sharp sickle
Clears the debris on a mountain.

AT SAKURAI VILLAGE

To my beloved child[ren]
My final message:
Flowers blooming
With all of their heart
In lovely Sakurai village.[4]

---

[4] This refers to the parting of the warrior Kusonoki Musashige (d. 1136) and his son Masatsura that took place in Sakurai. Masashige knew that he would not return alive from the fateful battle of Minatogawa, and bid his son farewell, comparing the life of a samurai to the cherry blossoms, glorious but short lived. It is likely Rengetsu is also alluding to her own dead children.

WATER BY AN OLD TEMPLE

The sound of pure water
Dripping down
The moist walls
Of the temple
Also proclaims the Law of Buddha.

WHISTLING KETTLE

Listen closely—
At this mountain temple,
The sound of the wind in the pines
And the whistle of a kettle
Are the voice of Buddha.

BLACKENED THING

Another year passes;
On my kitchen shelf
Something blackened with soot
I need to clean—
An image of Buddha.

UPON SEEING YOUNG NUNS ON THEIR BEGGING ROUNDS

Take your first steps
On the long path of the Way;
Please do not dream
Your lives away
Walk on to the end.

WHEN PEOPLE TEASE ME ABOUT MY CONSTANT CHANGE OF RESIDENCE

A floating cloud,
Drifting about
Playing my version
Of hide-and-seek—
Try to find me!

PEOPLE LAUGHED AT ME FOR DRESSING LIKE A BEGGAR

Yes, when you compare
My robe with others,
Mine is the shabbiest—
No one else looks
So ragged.

Yes , I am a beggar
Of verse:
Trying to pick out words
As if they were pearls
Of falling dew.

ONI[5]

Do not resist, [Mr. Oni]
Open the lotus inside
And overthrow
All the demons
In your heart.

---

[5] *Oni* are ferocious goblins that sometimes can be converted to Buddhism, transforming their demonic power into a force for good.

HEART

Coming and going,
Without beginning nor end
Like ever changing
White clouds
This heart of mine.

THE PLEASURES OF CALLIGRAPHY

Taking up the brush
Simply for the joy of it.
Writing on and on,
Leaving behind
Long lines of dancing letters.

INCENSE BURNER

A single line of
Fragrant smoke
From the incense stick
Trails off without a trace:
Where does it go?

A LIFE OF RETIREMENT

Reside in a living landscape
And it becomes yours:
Daikon dries along the fence,[6]
Trees full of chestnuts
Brush against the eaves of my hut.

---

[6] Daikon, a giant white radish, is a nourishing and tasty food that can be grown easily. Daikon is a staple of the Japanese diet that can be eaten raw, boiled, or pickled.

MOUNTAIN RETREAT

The roar of a waterfall
The howl of a
Mountain storm—
I am used to them shouting
At me until morning.

STORM
DEEP IN THE MOUNTAINS

The roar awakens me from
A peaceful slumber
Yet the fierce
Mountain wind also blows
Away the dust in my heart.

ON THE FIGHTING DURING
THE CIVIL WAR[7]

Ally or foe, winner and loser—
For all of them,
Nothing but pity,
When brother fights brother
In our beloved land.

To those who strike
And those who are struck
Keep this in your hearts:
Are we not all people
Of the same divine land?

---

[7] As the Tokugawa Shogunate tottered toward collapse in the 1860s, fierce fighting between Shogunate troops and loyalists seeking restoration of the imperial system of rule broke out around Kyoto. By legend, Rengetsu gave this poem to Saigo Takamori, leader of the loyalist troops, who took the message to heart, and negotiated a peaceful end to the war.

AMERICANS
WILL BE ARRIVING[8]

It is rumored that the Americans
Will be arriving with the spring rains—
No need to be disturbed,
It will refresh our land
With needed moisture.

---

[8] In 1854, Commodore Perry forcefully opened Japan to international trade, and negotiated the establishment of an American mission. Although many of Rengetsu's acquaintances belonged to the "Revere the Emperor, Expel the Barbarians!" movement, she was much more optimistic about the event. Rengetsu wrote many poems praising the restoration of the Emperor, taking it to be the dawning of a new age; as we see in this poem, she believed that the introduction of certain elements of world culture would be of benefit to Japan. (She was a particularly big fan of Western medicine.)

INSCRIPTION PLACED ON A PAINTING OF A COURTESAN

Even if you meet them
Only once
It is your lot
To promise them
To wait forever.

RANDOM THOUGHTS

Someday, I, too,
Will cross over;
In tonight's dream
I was on a floating bridge
Moving to the other shore.

When you are old,
You should sleep a lot—
Dreamland
Is the one place
You never age.

MOON OVER THE BRIDGE

Spanning the known
And the unknown past,
Bearing all the pathos
The world offers:
Moonlit Uji Bridge.

SPEAR BEARER[9]

Swaggering along
Single mindedly serving his lord:
The spear bearer strides ahead
As if meeting a lover
at Ausaka Gate.

---

[9] Spear bearers were vanguard of the spectacular processions that provincial lords were obliged to make to and from the shogun's capital of Edo. The spear bearers, brandishing long lances topped with feathers and animal fur, swaggered from side to side, lifting their legs high up into the air to attract attention. Ausaka (Osaka), "the slope where people meet," was an important checkpoint along the Tokaido.

FISHERMAN SINGS TO THE MOON

Rhythmically, he poles
In time to the music
Of his folk song:
A fisherman's little boat
Drenched in moonlight.

HUMBLE IN BODY
BUT PURE IN HEART

Bodies bent and shaky
But mountain folk
Always keep their
Minds as polished
As their sickles.

LIGHT OF THE DHARMA

If you want to
Spread the light
Of the Dharma,
Let it first illumine
Your own heart.

WHEN A THIEF CAME

If the mountain bandit
Came to my place
To steal away
Golden oak leaves
He struck it rich!

Not a trace
Of the thief
But he left behind
The peaceful stillness
Of the Okazaki Hills.

SAKE

Savor delicious sake
Without overdoing it
And it becomes
An elixir that eases
Old age and death.

MEMORIES OF MY HUSBAND

Together we enjoyed
These cherry blossoms,
And passed long summers
In the mountains:
Standing here, such sadness.

`

CELEBRATING THE PINE

The world's dust
Swept aside
No care for the future—
In my hermitage I have all I need:
The wind in the pines.

A LAST WISH

My last wish is
To die beneath the
Light of the autumn moon
So I will no longer be lost in
The darkness.

DEATH VERSE[10]

My hope for the afterworld:
To rest upon
A blooming lotus flower
Gazing at a full moon,
In a cloudless sky.

---

[10] It can be said that Rengetsu left three death poems: "Gazing Upon the Sky at Sunset" (34), "A Last Wish" (155), and the one given here. This one was written on a white shroud with a painting of a lotus and a moon on it by Tessai. Rengetsu was wrapped in the shroud upon her death and placed in her coffin.

Tales of
RENGETSU

THE MARTIAL ARTIST

During her tenure at Kameoka Castle, Nobu became adept at the martial arts, attaining instructor-level proficiency in a number of different weapon systems and jujutsu techniques. When Nobu and her female friends were out in the town, she thrashed would-be mashers with jujutsu arm locks and throws. Word spread that "Nobu is a great beauty, but don't try to accost her. She will kick your ass."

Even after the samurai lady Nobu became the nun Rengetsu, she practiced the martial arts on the side. Rengetsu taught jujutsu privately to local ladies, and others report that she practiced with wooden staff or sword. Priest Chiman witnessed Rengetsu jump over a three-foot fence holding a wooden staff in her hands when she was in her seventies.

Rengetsu was a master of disarming opponents. When she caught a thief attempting to break into Jinko-in, she asked him, "Looking for something? Let me show you around." The thief was so intimidated by the power of her presence that he meekly followed her out of the temple.

For Rengetsu, calligraphy was a martial art. In the martial arts, suki means "an opening," "a lack of focus," and "slackness in one's posture and confusion in one's mind." There is not a single suki present in Rengetsu's calligraphy. There is no mistaking that it is the brushwork of a powerful woman warrior. Throughout her life, Rengetsu maintained the demeanor of a martial artist.

ONE CANNOT BUY CULTURE

Rengetsu was a loyalist—one who supported the overthrow of the Tokugawa regime and the restoration of the emperor—so she avoided meeting Shogunate officials. She was in some danger of being arrested or even assassinated because she harbored loyalist opponents of the government. A high-ranking Shogunate official with a retinue came to her hut, requesting that she brush several tanzaku (thin poetry cards) for him. Rengetsu did not care for his haughty attitude, so she demurred. Then the official offered her a substantial amount of money. Still Rengetsu turned him down and proclaimed, "In our world it is impossible for one to buy culture." In other words, refinement is something that must be acquired slowly with good taste, not something that comes automatically with high office. Despite his entreaties, the official had to return home empty handed.

A NARROW ESCAPE

One night, an intruder broke into Rengetsu's hut. Rengetsu calmly told him, "If you can find money or anything else of value you are welcome to it." Rengetsu sat by the hibachi warming herself while she watched the robber ransack her closet. She gave him a large *furoshiki* to hold the items. Not only that, she told him, "If you have become a robber it means that you have nothing to eat. Let me cook you something." The robber replied, "I have no time for that." "Well, then," Rengetsu said, "I will make you some barley cakes from flour I received as a gift the other day." Rengetsu did so. The robber gobbled up the barley cakes and left.

Early the following morning, a farmer showed up at her door. "I found a dead man in my field. He was carrying a large furoshiki with your name on it, so I thought he was running an errand for you," he reported. Rengetsu said, "That must be that out-of-luck fellow that visited me late last night. I gave him some things I no longer needed and a furoshiki to carry them." The farmer realized that the dead man was a robber, not an errand boy.

When Rengetsu went to see the body, she recognized the man. She was greatly frightened to see that he had spit up a lot of blood. Officials were summoned, and it was determined that the man had been poisoned. Rengetsu was questioned in detail about the circumstances of the man's death a number of times, but all she could say was that, "I live alone, so people often give me food such as barley flour." No charges were filed, and the case was closed.

It was discovered that Rengetsu was the intended target of the poison. Due to her loyalist sympathies and connection with many of the main agitators, Rengetsu was considered a threat to the Shogunate. A stranger had given the poisoned flour to an old granny in the neighborhood to deliver to Rengetsu, who did not use the flour immediately. She only brought it out to feed the unfortunate robber.

RENGETSU-YAKI IMITATIONS

As Rengetsu-yaki became increasingly in demand, other potters decided to jump on the bandwagon and make imitations of her work. Rather than being upset about this occurrence, Rengetsu was nonchalant. "If it helps them make a living, it is fine with me." As mentioned, Rengetsu's calligraphy is inimitable, so some potters had the gumption to come to Rengetsu and ask, "We can more or less make pottery in your style but cannot copy your calligraphy. Would you mind adding your poems to our pieces?" Rengetsu did so with alacrity. She even went so far to tell imitators, "It is no good to sell only copies of my pottery. Let me give you a few genuine pieces to mix them together."

MARKET PRICE

In the beginning, there was no set price for Rengetsu's pottery. People gave what they could. One day, a wealthy customer left quite a tidy sum of money in a payment envelope. (In Japan, money is presented in an envelope to be opened later.) When Rengetsu discovered how much he had paid her, she became perturbed. If regular customers found out that Rengetsu's pottery was valued at such a high price, they would feel compelled to offer more money so that they would not look cheap. As a result, the market price would rise, and her work would be less affordable. Thereafter, Rengetsu established a fixed price for her wares, at the same cost for everyone.

TOO MUCH

So many people visited Rengetsu that she con-
tinually shifted her residence. Since people still
managed to find her, she posted a sign stating,
"Rengetsu is not at home," and hid inside her hut.
Admirers continually sent her provisions, far more
than she needed or could ever use. Rengetsu's hut
became a warehouse, so she had to redistribute its
contents to others. Since Rengetsu wore the sim-
plest and cheapest robes, the kind donned by crafts-
people, and never dressed up in Buddhist regalia, she
was at a loss when presented with fine clothes. She
was equally distressed by large donations of cash. She
wondered, "What am I going to do with so much

money?" Rengetsu returned the money with a letter of appreciation for the gift but added, "For someone like me who has abandoned the world, money is a hindrance, not an asset."

THE COPYWRITER

It is tradition for a merchant to have a well-known calligrapher brush the logo for his or her product. The famous poet Ryokan brushed the signboard for Joshu-ya, a maker of soy products, three times. It kept getting stolen because of the beautiful calligraphy. Yamaoka Tesshu, swordsman, Zen master, and calligrapher, brushed signboards that still can be seen today in various parts of Tokyo, such as "Tesshu Noodles," and "Kimura Bakery."

There was an old lady named Horiuchi Kane who ran a shop selling *sakuramochi*. (*Sakuramochi* is a sweet rice cake wrapped in a leaf from a cherry tree.) Horiuchi thought that it would be a great help with sales if she could have a Rengetsu poem reproduced on the paper cover over the rice cakes. When she approached Rengetsu with the idea, Rengetsu came up with this advertising copy:

> Buy one!
> It has the lofty name of
> Mountain Cherry Blossom,
> This rice cake made with feeling,
> Wrapped in a fresh leaf.

DO IT RIGHT!

When Rengetsu was living at Jinko-in, the acolyte monks practiced chanting the Buddhist sutras in the temple next door. If one of them stumbled over a phrase or forgot the words, Rengetsu, who was working on calligraphy or making pottery in her tea room, called out in a piercing martial-art shout, "That is not correct! Do it again until you get it right!"

TEACHER OF COURTESANS

Three famed courtesans of the era—Sakuragi Tayu, Ueda Chikako, and Miwa Teishin—were Rengetsu's disciples.

Sakuragi (n.d.) was the Tayu (star courtesan) of the Wachigaiya Teahouse in the Shimabara pleasure quarters. She was said to have been extraordinarily beautiful, called "The Flower of Kyoto." Two of her lovers were central players in the Meiji Restoration: Katsura Kogoro (also known as Kido Takayoshi, 1833–1877) and Ito Hirofumi (1841–1909). Katsura, later to become an imperial advisor, was her patron in her early years. Sakuragi then fell in love with Ito—one of the key figures of the era, who eventually served as Prime Minister four times—and became his mistress. Sakuragi is the model for Ito, the heroine geisha of the popular novel and television drama Wachigaiya Ito. Following the 1909 assassination of Ito in Korea, Sakuragi became a nun and spent the rest of her days in seclusion. Sakuragi often visited Rengetsu for instruction in poetry and calligraphy. She sometimes signed her poems "Sakuragi, disciple of Rengetsu."

Ueda Chikako (professional name O-Kaji, ?–1894) was born in the Gion pleasure quarters. She become a maiko at 12 years old and began her study of waka at an early age. Chikako became known as the "Poet Courtesan of the Gion." When one of her teachers Nagasawa Tomoo (1808–1859) committed suicide in jail, she considered becoming a nun. Rengetsu dissuaded her: "Taking vows as a nun is not for you. You have more work to do for the people of your country." Chikako lived near Rengetsu for a time and frequently went to Rengetsu's hut. In her later years, Chikako had many waka students of her own and published several collections of her poetry.

Miwa Teishin (1809–1902) was the daughter of the potter Aoki Kibei (1767–1833). She became one of the most popular geisha of Gion. Teishin was ransomed by a rich clothing merchant, but after he died, she became a nun. Teishin was an accomplished poet of both haiku and waka. Teishin established a school that she named Bright Wind Academy.

All three courtesans regularly visited Rengetsu for instruction in poetry and calligraphy, advice on life, and inspiration. They wanted to be like Rengetsu— artistic, refined, and full of unyielding spirit.

JUST IN CASE

Rengetsu had a carpenter friend who visited her from time to time. One day Rengetsu said to him, "Please make a coffin for me." When the carpenter asked why, she replied, "I have become old and frail, so you never know when I will die. Prepare a coffin for me just in case." The carpenter did as Rengetsu requested and brought it to her place. Until the end of her days, Rengetsu used the container to store rice, and when she died it did become her coffin.

LIST OF ARTWORK

The images featured in this publication are reproductions of original Rengetsu art, unless otherwise specified. All are used with permission from the following contributors:

The Kaeru-an Collection
Photographs by Felix Hess

Page 19: *Rengetsu's Hut and Pine Tree* accompanied by the poem:

> Living deep in the mountain
> I have grown fond of the
> Sound of murmuring pines;
> On days the wind does not blow,
> How lonely it is!

Page 39: *Eggplants*. Detail from painting.

John Stevens
Photographs by John Stevens

Page 5: *Rengetsu's Hut in Nishigamo,* painted by Tomioka Tessai. From *Ama no Karumo,* published by Saneido, Kyoto. 1870. Public domain.

Page 32: *Basket of Fresh Greens.* (Final artwork by Rengetsu created two days before death.) Painting by Tomioka Tessai, poem by Rengetsu:

> Going down to the Kamo River
> To wash the fresh greens
> That I have gathered this morning,
> In a willow along the bank
> I hear an uguisu sing.

The Private Collection of Dr. John Fong and Dr. Colin Johnstone
Photographs by Dr. John Fong

Cover: *Plum Tree with Calligraphy.*

Page 11:   *Rengetsu's Hut.* Detail from painting.

Page 13:   *Uguisu and Plum Blossoms* accompanied by the poem:

> When the uguisu
> Come to the capital
> I'd like one to visit
> My favorite plum tree
> To enjoy the fragrant blossoms.

Page 16:   *Pine Tree.* Detail from painting.

Page 25:   *The Moon Over Akashi Bay.* Detail from hand scroll.

Page 37:   *Autumn Moon.* Detail from painting.

Page 61:   *Lotus.* Detail from painting.

Page 125: *Uji Bridge.* Detail from painting.

Page 161: *Seasonal Plates.* Rengetsu-yaki.

Page 163: *Cylindrical Wall Vase.* Rengetsu-yaki.

Page 165 *Teapot.* Rengetsu-yaki.

Page 167: *Gourd-shaped Wall Vase.* Rengetsu-yaki.

Page 169: *Tanuki Incense Holder.* Rengetsu-yaki.

Page 171: *Sake Flask.* Rengetsu-yaki.

Page 172: *Four Tea Cups with Original Box signed by Rengetsu.*
Rengetsu-yaki.

Robyn Buntin of Honolulu Gallery

Page 41: *Billowing Willow Branch*. Detail from painting.

Page 85: *Chrysanthemum*. Detail from painting.

Page 109: *Pine Tree*. Detail from painting.

Page 157: *Teapot and Cups*. Detail from painting.

Page 159: *Martial Art Teacup*. Rengetsu-yaki with incised poem:

> The bow shaped moon
> Reminds me of the brave warrior
> In the Battle of Yashima Bay
> Who would not let his bow
> Float away in the tide.[1]

Page 166: *Incense Burner*. Rengetsu-yaki.

Page 175: *Tea Bowl*. Rengetsu-yaki.

---

[1] This refers to a story in the *Tale of the Heike*. During a fierce battle at Yashima Bay, Minamoto no Yoshitsune accidentally dropped his bow in the sea. He dived into the deep water to retrieve it. When the other samurai asked him why he risked his life for a bow he said, "The bow was strung for a weak archer, and if it washed up on the enemy's shore, they would get the impression that our entire force was weak. I could not dishonor our side like that."

RESOURCES

For regularly updated blog posts on the life and artwork of Otagaki Rengetsu and a complete list of references in both English and Japanese, please visit *The Rengetsu Circle* on the Robyn Buntin of Honolulu website: *www.RobynBuntin.com*.

Further information on the collection of Dr. Fong and Dr. Johnstone can be found at *www.RengetsuZenCollections.com*.

ABOUT JOHN STEVENS

John Stevens lived in Japan for 35 years where he was Professor and Aikido Instructor at Tohoku Fukushi University in Sendai. He has written dozens of books on all aspects of Asian culture, and acted as curator for several major exhibitions of Zen art. Other titles by John Stevens available from Echo Point Books are *The Marathon Monks of Mt. Hiei*, *Sacred Calligraphy of the East*, *The Philosophy of Aikido*, and *Extraordinary Zen Masters*.

Pictured above: Author John Stevens at Rengetsu's hut on the grounds of Jinko-in in Kyoto. (Photograph by Mei Hosho.)

CPSIA information can be obtained at www.ICGtesting.com
Printed in the USA
BVOW02s0118310715

410877BV00012B/21/P

9 781626 549319